How to Make a Guy Fall in Love with You And Remain Faithful Forever.

Just for Girls

By Carlisle Woods

DEDICATION

I wish to dedicate this book to two groups of individuals; my family: Emmy, Runi, Roro and Rayon, Chazzy, and Shay; and to all the girls who have been seeking for true love, but have not found it yet. I also wish to thank everyone else who has helped me to have a better understanding of the nature and dynamics of relationships between men and women.

CONTENTS

ACKNOWLEDGMENTS

I have seen many couples falling quickly and strongly in love, only to separate shortly afterwards. I also know of girls who waited never-endingly to meet the right partner, then in desperation married someone different than they ever imagined; and others more who choose to remain single rather than compromise their ideals of who constitutes a good man.

However, there is no need for an impasse between you and an adorable man--if you know the secrets of successful dating.

Notwithstanding the myths about the scarcity of good men, I believe that genuine women can find and keep good relationships with wonderful men, who are still in plentiful supply; but you need to know where to find them, how to engage them, and how to motivate them to commit to you.

The forthcoming material is an amplification of a conversation with a friend who was seeking to find a soul mate but had not succeeded so far. Then I realized that meeting men and forming relationships with them could be challenging for many women. The conversation that follows can be of great help to any girl who faces these challenges.

The ideas will reveal how men generally assess women's words and actions; suggest how women can motivate men to chase after them. They will also help women to boost their self-esteem, identify marriageable men, and recognize evasive ones who shirk from making long-term commitments.

Generally, these suggestions will help women to develop the karma that will motivate men to pursue them. So say goodbye to loneliness and hello to an exciting friendship with a terrific man who will love

HOW TO MAKE A GUY FALL IN LOVE WITH YOU AND REMAIN FAITHFUL FOREVER

and   adore   you   forever.

1 Getting Ready to Date

At a family function, I asked an unmarried friend how close she was to tying the knot. She replied:

"I'm looking for a guy, but I haven't found one yet."

Wide-eyed, with a curious smirk and a jittery tone I replied, men are hunters; they like to chase women—not be chased by them.

"Oh yeah! Why haven't I found any yet?

I'll tell you why. Maybe you are looking in the wrong places or at the wrong men, or maybe your expectations are unrealistic. I know that you are looking for the best available man, but none will ideally fit your mold.

"Hmmm… That is interesting! Continue."

Women's desire for male companionship churns from various motives, such as conquest, sexual exhilaration, social acceptance, or a sense of achievement. However, many women are seeking a lifelong attachment to a marriageable man whom they can set up family with.

"Ok"

Understanding how men think and how they evaluate women is a subject not yet included on school curricula, so girls learn the art mainly through their experiences with men and advice from their girlfriends. However, hearts often break in the process of falling in love. Having the skills to identify and keep a good man is necessary if you wish to establish the traditional family structure, or keep your marriage intact—if you are already married. Additionally, your window of fertility may close, or you might become a single parent before acquiring successful dating skills. I will therefore share some ideas about the way men generally assess and tackle women, so that you will not be flustered unnecessarily, or contrarily, misinterpret and sketch false stereotypes of them. The suggestions will also help women in general to know themselves better, and know how to respond appropriately to men's antics.

"All right, I'm listening"

Many marriageable men are available, but you have to capture their attention before even getting to the point of forming a significant friendship. Men are also looking for fine girls to marry and setup families with, but they too are having difficulties identifying suitable ones. The problem then, on both sides of the fence, is not just a shortage of good men and women, but a short supply of the skills to identify and attract those who qualify. Inasmuch as men and women have a mutual need for each other, the process of selection gets knotty due to contemporary changes of moral ethics. The traditional one-man-to-one-woman marriage has declined markedly due to an increasing acceptance of same-sex marriage. Nonetheless, eligible men still exist, though it requires specific skills to find and keep them.

Repeatedly, men hurt women by exploiting their vulnerabilities and treating them as temporary hookups. However, men may not be completely culpable for treating women as such, because women subconsciously abet some of their negative treatments through two extremes: subservience on one hand, and aggression on the other. Subservience is often a woman's means to convey affection and arrest a man's affection, whereas aggression is a spillover from desperation. Woman is man's equal—not his servant or his lord. If a woman worships a man, he is likely to lose his appeal for her; if she bullies him, he escapes her hounding. Both of these polarities are probably the effects of having more women than men who are seeking intimate relationships. However, there is still hope for all the women who are looking to find good husbands!

"I see! Now tell me, what can I do to make a guy attract towards me?"

Finding the right man by coincidence is an extreme unlikelihood, and considering the risks of dating a complete stranger, you need to sketch a profile of the qualities that you are looking for in a mate, and then create a strategy that would expose you to possibilities. Your choice will inevitably affect every facet of your life and your children's thereafter. Various types of men are available, but you need to find the species that will stand with you through the twist and turns of life.

Equally important to finding Mr. Right is to be an amazing girl yourself. People are generally anxious about *getting* premium product, but they seem less inclined to *give* the same. It is only fair to want a good spouse if you determine to be good yourself.

"No problem, I'm a good girl!"

I believe. Ok, here is my plan. Wide area prospecting is complicated and risky; therefore, waving your antenna within some specific territories favors success. If you were hungry, you would go to a restaurant. Finding a soul mate is similar in some ways, because no one knocks on doors inquiring for eligible women. If you want to find a husband, you have to be at places where someone can find you.

"This sounds like a good idea. Can you

explain how to do this?"

Sure. Participation in an interesting hobby or an educational activity expands your horizon and gives you the opportunity to meet either, men whom you might find your match among, or girls who might introduce you to an eligible friend or family member. Thus, your chances of finding a soul mate increase, as your network of friends gets larger. You can also create circles as a means to expand your friendship network.

Circles! What do you mean?

Let me explain. Circles are clusters of friends that you establish relationships with through social events like ice skating, bowling, camping, or scrabble, etcetera. You can create several of these circles in different areas of your life, such as work, school, church, or the neighborhood. These circles will provide traffic for you to intercept people of common interest, and they have the potential to get bigger and bigger as your friends continue to introduce you to their friends—like a chain reaction or a domino effect. Businesspersons agree that you have to spend money to make money. Similarly, you must expend efforts to develop friendships; and whilst unassumingly interfacing with others, you are much more likely to encounter and fall in love with Prince Charming.

Now, it happens often that compatible men and women exist within common spheres, so you must find a way of intercepting someone who might qualify as a good soul mate. We have already talked about creating collision traffic for social interaction, but transforming the relationship into love requires a little initiative, such as moving slowly from superficial talk to more in-depth issues, which elucidate feelings, emotions, values, and aspirations. This second level of communication is the eye that sees into the other's heart. Upon reaching this point, you must sensibly decide whether to keep driving, or to get off at the next exit—if you sense danger.

"Interesting, go on."

Your eagerness to hitch must not obscure your assessment of personality. Inasmuch as you are anxious and ready to settle down, you must be conscientious about making an intelligent choice.

"Of course! However, right now I do not have much time left, seeing that I am getting older by the moment. I've got to be on top of my game to make it happen as quickly as possible."

Sounds like you are ready to get aggressive here; however, there are some drawbacks with being pushy. First, a man will repulse a girl who searches desperately for a husband because he believes that an anxious woman will grab easily at any available man, and then leave for another one who seems superior to him. Attraction between boy and girl has to balance mutually. The likelihood that your friendship will thrive depends whether each partner contributes equally to the bond. Whenever one party-- particularly the girl--shows greater interest, the man is likely to put her on a back burner.

"Really; are you saying that a man gets choosy whenever the girl is panicky about getting hitched?"

Bingo! Desperation can drive a girl to take drastic measures to achieve her goals, and any apparent anxiety discourages admirers. It is only natural for a girl who is growing older to experience some frustration, but showing it overtly lowers her ability to attract an eligible bachelor.

Women are becoming more and more ambitious, and they back it up with fists and brains—by working and studying hard, and then earning good salaries and high social statuses. However, an increasingly popular species of parasitic men attract towards these successful women for sex and swing. Do not panic! You can blow their cover easily if you hear them offering excuses like these: "I forgot my wallet"; "I don't have any change"; "there must be a mistake with my credit card"; "I'm going to the bathroom" (when it's time to pay), etcetera. Parasites eventually destroy their hosts, and then find new ones. Watch out for these men, because they seldom linger after you have satisfied their curiosities.

So now, as the number of marriageable men shrinks, women are 'swinging' frantically to score home runs—finding husbands--but their swings are neutralizing men's enthusiasm to go after them. Why would a man stress over wowing a girl, if easy ones hit on him constantly? Men are hunters; they love adventure; they enjoy chasing after women; they love girls who are not easy. Girls ought to put men back on the hunter's trail!

"Ok, so frustration is a no-no. What if I treat him like a prince; would he become fonder of me?"

Respecting him and his ideals is commendable, but pampering or hoisting him on a pedestal can inflate his ego and spoil him—similarly to a spoilt child whom its parents pamper. Moreover, treating him in a motherly or sisterly manner can make him tag you as family, loose his romantic appeal for you, then 'shop' elsewhere.

"Are you suggesting a kind of standoffish approach?"

Not exactly! I am merely saying that you should never put a halo over a man, nor give him an over-impression that you are the lucky one. Girls particularly merit these compliments, because they are the gems whom men are seeking. Remember, God created Adam first, and then He created Eve for him to love and treasure. She was God's gift to Adam; and you are God's gift to a lucky man. You also do not need to feel guilty about being single now. Different girls establish friendships at different ages and stages in their lives, and furthermore, many who married early confessed later on that they had not made intelligent choices.

"If I happen to meet a wonderful guy, should I try to accelerate the friendship so that we can get hitched as quickly as possible?"

Desperation is a ghost that scares admirers. It is important to 'cool out' whenever you are looking for a husband, therefore, allowing the man to set the pace for the relationship will give him a sense of control—an opportunity that men generally appreciate. It does not mean that you would be statically submissive to all of his wishes throughout the entire courtship, because as it progresses, you will find many opportunities to negotiate mutually agreeable compromises. However, if you are pushy in regards to an early marriage, his interest is likely to weaken. Time is a critical component, because it affords you the opportunity to discern pungent matters that can ferment later on.

Fascination is the magnet that pulls a couple together at first, but love is the glue that binds both. Many women wished they were yet single and free of the problems of an unhappy marriage. Because it is easy to fall in love with someone whom you spend quality time with, it would be wise to spread out your dates so that you have sufficient time for reflection and assessment, and consequently avoid infatuation. Taken for granted that marriage represents a permanent union between a man and a woman, how can you carelessly hop into it without considering the fitness of the one whom you wish to marry and live with forever?

"That is quite true! Another question: Can I tell whether or not a man loves me genuinely?"

As a seeking woman, you should try to determine at an early stage whether or not your date has genuine concerns for your wellbeing, and if he is good material. Here are some suggestions that will help you to make these determinations.

Love and lust are two completely different characters, but you can easily confuse their identities because lust often dresses up in love's costumes. Nevertheless, you can tell the difference between them if you carefully examine their behavior over time. Love has a spirit of giving, whereas lust specializes on receiving. Love puts other persons before it, seeks to please them, and never tires of waiting for the right moment to celebrate. Love is also willing to settle disputes politely, whereas lust catches a fit, barks at you, and then slams the door in your face if you question its authority.

Love is like a plant that grows slowly and fertilizes through compassionate acts, tender words, and a sacred regard for your thoughts and feelings. It blossoms when a couple socializes in a variety of settings—not just in a small bubble. Therefore, going into the open environment and doing amusing things together will help you to make a realistic evaluation of his personality. The way he treats other people whom he casually interacts with is exactly the way he would treat you when the initial attraction wears off.

When a man loves you, he will make you the centerpiece of his attention, and will demonstrate a willingness to make compromises for the benefit of mutual happiness. He will adjust his schedule to spend more time with you and will give you royal treatment whenever you are out together. He will also respect your opinions, be coordinated with your feelings and emotions, and demonstrate an aptitude to enliven your spirits whenever you are edgy. Moreover, he will endeavor to fulfill your needs above his own, keep his promises, and never force you to do things that are contrary to your scruples. Additionally, he will not be in any rush to sleep with you, since he intends to marry you sometime soon.

Although love often expresses itself through the above common courtesies, you must never take them as foolproof confirmation. Always measure these gestures against your gut feelings, and your friends' and family's opinion and advice.

Sheer charm is not all that a girl needs to motivate a man to marry her. This man might dispense just enough affection to keep her hanging on to his coattail, whilst he has no intention to move the relationship further. If he is not marriage material in the first instance, this girl is simply wasting her time.

"Are you serious?"

Yep! A man is on a different timeline than a woman since he has no window of fertility, and therefore he does not jitter about settling down. Thus, in addition to sheer love, he must also be prepared to start the journey of togetherness, least you spend the rest of your life in limbo.

"Is it possible to differentiate between good men and players?"

Shiftiness and evasiveness characterize players, and they loathe letting other people into their emotions. These men are difficult to identify due to their fancy exterior façade, which serves as a camouflage for luring girls. People generally assess merchandise by the packaging, and most often, the wrap belies the true contents. Thus, it is risky to assess a man by examining his external qualities. Therefore, a girl should try as soon as possible—before she falls too deeply in love--to understand the psychology of the man who is trying to 'take her breath away'.

Men in general like to be physically intimate, but unlike good-intentioned ones, evasive men prefer to be emotionally detached, because superficiality helps him to cope with separation, which he anticipates soon, since he does not intend to stay around forever. The fear of emotional transparency is suggestive of his inability to be faithful. Consequently, many tentative relationships exist nowadays! For instance, a man might have a girlfriend in every city that he visits for business, or a girl might have several boyfriends—some as backups in the event that one or the other leaves. Thus, culture and phobia have morphed people into being light lovers, who shy away from making lifelong commitments. There is no quick fix for this type of problem, except knowing yourself, whom you are seeking, and having a plan to achieve your goals. The avoidant man who fears emotional intimacy usually finds it easy to engage sexually with an outsider whom it is unlikely he would make a commitment to. For him, infidelity is a freedom spree that detaches him emotionally from the girl he is currently dating, and who threatens to get emotionally close to him. Being extremely flirtatious, evasive men often hop from one relationship to another, since they thrive with support from several hosts. Beware!

"Huh, no kidding!"

Secondly, when a man's marketable skills are low, he is unemployed, or he earns substantially less than his partner earns, he subconsciously squats into a low self-esteem posture, during which time his threatened masculine identity tempts him to have affairs with other women. Couples with similar educational and financial moorings do comparatively better at maintaining relationships than those who differ markedly on these bases.

"Let me ask you another question. Would my date get jealous easily if I keep in touch with male friends form high school, or with someone whom I dated previously?"

Interesting question! A good man is careful about who gets close to his woman, and so he is always protective in this regard. Usually, he would share anything but her, period!

"Glad to hear this, women neither!"

Therefore, it is quite natural for him to get jealous if she divides her interest between other men and him. Very rarely would he fret if she spends time with her girlfriends, but a close male friendship makes him edgy, and threatens the security of the relationship. Whereas an over possessive man will isolate you from everyone, a good man only feels threatened when you show over-excitement about these old acquaintances. Therefore, although you can still keep in touch with 'oldies', having some clear boundaries will avert suspicions that you treasure memories of them.

"What else can I do to be more eligible?"

Presentation and self-esteem are two correlated themes that can affect a girl's luck, so let us talk abut them.

2 Presentation and Self Esteem

To find Prince Charming--or more appropriately stated--to have him find you-- you must first arrest his attention by the way you present yourself. Three integral components of presentation are dress, adornment, and deportment. Though these attributes may not necessarily reveal your personality, they are the litmus by which others assess you. Devious girls often get high ratings and quick proposals than cool girls do, because they present themselves elegantly. This happens so because external beauty first attracts a man. Afterwards, charisma and other fine qualities will keep him connected, but you must first arrest his attention with a charming persona. It follows then, that when a cool girl fails to present herself attractively, she hinders men from admiring her.

Moreover, dress and intellectual growth should complement each other. Being visually oriented, men rouse easily by sensual dress, and they are likely to confront you with a posture that your fashion incites. Over-reveling attire attracts a man to the woman's body—not necessarily to her person. Even men in relationships attract easily by provocative attire on the premise of base 'Visio-sexual' instinct. Vision is the portal to passion—the heart digests and assimilates what the eyes chew on. Therefore, if a woman dresses conservatively, men will approach her respectfully, whereas if she dresses provocatively, men might confront her impolitely. Sensual dress then has a subtle way of trifling with the inner qualities that you value and wish to personify.

Additionally, sensual attire makes you the core of attraction wherever you are; and undoubtedly, you will command numerous neck turns, raised eyebrows, and whistles; however, if you were serious about finding true love, it would be difficult to identify Mister Right from a squadron of admirers.

Over-revealing attire can make a good-intentioned man consider you as just an ordinary person, and although he might pursue, his attraction might purely be on the premise of physical stimulus, which thrill is typically short-lived.

In order for others to adore you for psyche instead of physique, it is important to dress in a manner that conveys such priority.

For the most part, voluptuous dress kindles lust in the admirer's heart and shifts the spotlight away from your inner beauty. When it comes to dress, modesty is a good policy.

Body language, composure, and facial expression also give cues about your self-confidence. Smiling reacts positively on your moods, makes people around you feel accepted, and exerts a magnetic attraction; so you should get into the habit of smiling to others as much as possible. Smooth gait, elegant dress, pleasant smiles, and a good attitude will undoubtedly work in your favor.

"So you're saying that I should smile, smile, and smile?"

Oh yes, it really works, because it tells others that you are happy with yourself. I am not suggesting that you put on a phony one; be real, but be nice. Other people might not always be courteous, as you would like them to be; however, if you focus on the positive things in your life, your personality will gradually transform into one that delights others. Thus, self-presentation, although not the barometer of character, is the passport to opportunities.

"What do you think about being a macho girl? I grew up robustly, and I am capable of doing boyish stuff. Should I continue to be macho, or be more feminine?"

Wow! Difficult question; anyway this is what I think. Masculine agility can brew a measure of fear in a prospective wooer's mind, especially if he is not the macho type. Therefore, girls should generally allow men to do things that they are physically and traditionally adept to perform. Some examples are changing a car tire, pushing a trolley at the hardware, and climbing a ladder to repair a leaking gutter. Although it is wise to have working knowledge of these skills, you should keep them for emergencies, because allowing the man to do these chores will bolster his masculinity.

You might even be 'savvier' about certain

male related subjects than your date is, or be better talented at performing a male sport. However, waving your macho-manly banner in his face might just make you hang out alone for a long time.

Generally, men like to protect women; therefore denying your date the privilege of caring for you makes him feel unimportant. Nevertheless, you must avoid conceding your strength to over-dependency, or making him the kingpin of your happiness, because a dip of his loyalty can plunge you into despair. A delicate balance then, between independence and codependence is one of the keys to maintaining good relationships.

"This sounds fair. What is the next step? Am I ready to go 'shopping'?"

I think you are almost ready. Just a couple of things more.

"Ok."

Finding a man might be a relatively easy task, but deciding whether he is good stock, and sustaining the relationship after the friendship forms, present greater challenges. More than merely being a terrific and exciting guy, he should also be the kind who will remain in the driver's seat when the track gets bumpy. However, his mind-set and manners are not the only players in the relationship game; your self-evaluation and general life approach are critically important, because he can only see you through the lens of your self-esteem.

"So how can I enhance self-esteem?"

Glad you asked. Let me explain.

Outward actions reveal the inner picture of yourself; therefore, the way you are treated will depend on the way you conduct yourself since people can only see your outward behavior. The blueprints for personality etch during childhood;

therefore, the parents' early interaction with a girl shapes her self-esteem and the way she relates to others. Furthermore, if she were reared without a father, or with an abusive one, she catches a fractured portrait of manliness--what a man's role is, how he should treat women, and how she should respond to men. She might even feel some discomfort whenever she begins to get emotionally close to a man, simply because she has had little interaction with men.

Secondly, the vulnerability that accompanies childhood makes a young girl innocently trusting of adults, and she tends to believe whatever they tell her--verbally and non-verbally, and whether true or false. However, the notion that her character will hopelessly lock into a stereotype, with no prospects of reprieve, is false. With the proper tools, she can swerve from a negative trail onto a bright path. Self-esteem does not swing on the hinge of personal achievements or the lack thereof, past mistakes, or people's opinion of you.

"So what are the bases of self-esteem?"

Self-esteem revolves on God's estimate of your life, and your acknowledgement of His unconditional care--irrespective of feelings or foibles. A girl robs herself of true womanhood when she lets other people, or her personal feelings define her worth. If you have a low self-esteem, you will most surely gravitate towards an abusive man who will treat you in a manner that your actions and mind-set invite.

Feelings swerve from one state to another on a momentary scale, and so, grounding your personal worth on them will cause sporadic shifts from worthlessness to worthiness, and vice versa. However, believing that God loves you unconditionally, irrespective of your feelings and your circumstances, is the prescription to having a healthy self-esteem. An entire chain of effects precipitates whenever you envision yourself as a precious child of God; and as you begin to think and act as one, people's opinion of you will change, and they will treat you more politely. Thus, your enhanced self-esteem comes as a product of God's estimation of you; and the way you dress, walk, talk, and think, will transform due to having a positive self-worth, and not as the means to achieve one. At this point, you will not attempt to fabricate artificial gestures for others to accept you, because you now have an abiding assurance of God's love.

"Are you saying that self-esteem directly affects my likelihood of hitching?

Yep, but there is more to it. Negotiating and sustaining relationships is more intricate than you imagine, and having the required skills will give you an advantage. Critically important is that you acknowledge yourself as a masterpiece of God's creation and a unique blend of brains and beauty, and as such, you deserve every wonderful gift that the creator delights to bestow upon you.

However, simply mulling over this makeover without backing it up with fists will yield unsatisfactory results. After accepting yourself as God evaluates you, you should participate in social and educational programs that facilitate the growth of this positive image.

Moreover, every girl should first be comfortable in her own skin before attempting to bring cheerfulness to others, or trying to find someone to cheer her up. Trusting others and being kind to them is a good place to begin, however, since not everyone will respond favorably to your friendliness, you must be able to ride over occasional incidents of ingratitude.

Marrying and raising children is a dream

that most young women have, and achieving this goal is not very different from accomplishing educational and career goals; but success in any of these fields comes only by painstaking efforts and sacrifices. I have heard success defined as failure turned inside out, and therefore, the amount of success one enjoys often matches the efforts that one expends in pursuit of the goals.

"How is achieving success related to finding a husband?

If you believe that experience molds character, and that attitude affects success, then your chances of finding a good husband will either increase or reduce by the way you blend experience and attitude. Quite frequently, people deride the process of achieving success by riveting on the outcome, thereby missing the lessons that the process can teach. Like everything else in life, you might lose at relationships sometimes--a 'good' man may hand you a crocked deal, so you must have the mettle to bounce back and start all over again. Let me tell you about the Prodigal son (Luke 15:11-32) who initially made some poor decisions, but who make an astonishing recovery later on by deciding to return home. At the beginning of the story he was in a haste to receive his inheritance, but having not labored for it; he ran off and squandered the wealth that his father had painstakingly worked to amass. This mischievous son lacked the common sense to use the inheritance judiciously. However, he caught a new perspective of life whilst still dressed in rags and feeding pigs, and amazingly, he made a remarkable recovery after acknowledging the possibility of change. The Prodigal's experience also teaches a lesson of patience: things that come too quickly and too easily can be lost as readily as you acquire them. The prodigal had not matured psychologically to handle the inheritance. It belonged to him legally, but ignorance of its real worth forfeited him the proceeds that a shrewd management of it could procure. Two major choices confronted him: either he could have it immediately—with the risk of loss, or wait until he matured more, at which time he could shrewdly invest it to accumulate more wealth. Sometimes it pays to wait!

One should not let circumstances dictate one's destiny. Probably you are currently experiencing some challenges, but if you concentrate on your goals and maintain a positive spirit, you would ultimately reap success. Experience offers first-hand knowledge of the workable and the unworkable, and it is still the best teacher, though it presents tests before lessons.

"But everyone seems happy doing their own thing, with nothing to worry about.
However, here I am, lonely and frustrated, with no one to share my life."

I see! However, do not let other people's seeming happiness fool you, because many of them might be masking behind congeniality mascara. Falling in love merely to quell your insecurities or satisfy your fantasies courts disaster. Love ought to spring from a pure fountain. On the other hand, some women fear rejection by men, so they shirk dating. However, if they happen to date, they simply avoid emotional transparency by inviting physical play. Hold on! These tactics boomerang with double-pronged stings: either they attract evasive men who will never commit to marriage, or they give men license to treat such women as temporary hookups. Either way, girls who play these games will be the biggest losers—if marriage and family life are on their agenda. Genuine love is risky business—I know, and it makes girls vulnerable, but nonetheless it is an amazing experience.

Beware however, that marriage of itself will not hand you happiness. Some of the seemingly happy women that you see every day wished they were still single and free of the troubles of an unhappy marriage. If you are not happy and contented in your singleness, it is unlikely that marriage will affect a turnaround. Happiness qualifies you for companionship, but it is not the product of having things and people in your life, since many rich people are often miserable.

If you nitpick other people's faults constantly, they will inevitably avoid being around you; and shifting personal injury onto them will not mend your insecurities— it only alienates others. Thus, fixing the person in the mirror before fixing others is a good medicine for curing infections that often plague relationships.

"I do not have a problem with anyone who is different than me; however, I am not very lenient towards men who take women for

granted."

One physical law states that to every action there is an equal and opposite reaction. If we apply this principle to relationships, we might infer that our treatment of others translates into the way they treat us. Thus, coping with an eventual spouse requires the patience to tolerate his dissimilarities, affirm his strengths, and make allowances for his faults; bearing in mind that no one is perfect.

"Ok, I have a lot of this self-image and trust stuff covered. Let me ask another question. Would education affect my chances of finding a husband?"

Good question; it looks like you have been preparing for an encounter for some time now. Spending huge sums of money on physical accessories whilst giving little attention to mental improvement hinders your ability to comprehend others, as well as to articulate your ideas to them; therefore, you would do wisely to invest some resources on education, which boosts your confidence, earns the respect of others, and returns decent financial benefits in the end. Have you ever pondered why a seemingly unattractive woman weds a terrific man, and you wonder if she kidnapped him? I am not sure about that. However, if kidnapping is not the case, then unquestionably it took more than her looks to captivate him. Remember, when external beauty fades, intelligence still lingers, so put some labor into educating yourself.

Doing something new can be exciting, invigorating, and rewarding. It might simply be an upgrade in your area of expertise, a photography course, swimming lessons, or exercising at the gym. You might even enroll in music lessons, or gross anatomy. Reading the papers and viewing television news are also good habits because they keep you abreast with current events, provide conversation menus, and bolster your confidence whenever you dialogue with people. Therefore, whatever your preference is, do things that kindle enthusiasm and which can motivate others to do exciting things also.

"Sometimes I feel inclined to lounge in bed with my favorite snacks, because it compensates for the lack of having someone in my life."

Tada, here you go! A pity party will not do you any good—it only agitates you dilemma.

The lack of proper motivation can drive you to over indulge in appetite, until the habit becomes a trade-off for underachievement in the social and educational dimensions of your life, which eventually might lead to obesity or a gastro-related infirmity.

"I see; ok I'll take note of that. Hey Carlisle,

what is your opinion about utilizing one of the dating websites to find a match; I have seen some good results advertised on television?"

Huh? You might have different opinions about this, but this is what I think.

3 Online Dating

Online dating has become so trendy nowadays that people consider you as old-fashioned if you are not a digital junkie. Folk browse for mates on the internet as they do for regular merchandise; but when the product is also the sales person, how can shoppers assure themselves that they will get what they see advertised. Advertisers exaggerate the fine points on the upper surface, while the rusts conceal underneath. However, the eyes of old-fashioned courtship can perceive, more efficiently, both sides of someone's personality simultaneously. Have you noticed any difference between the profile photo and the living sample?

I believe that digital dating short-circuits the courtship experience, because emotions skew easily over Wi-Fi and coaxial cable. Although 'digidating' can provide a type of tarmac to launch a relationship, frail 'thrust' can hamper takeoff, and later on, furious 'tail winds' might force a crash landing.

Girls particularly are vulnerable to develop emotional attachment to men who mask behind technological blinds such as Face book, Twitter, Text messaging, and E-mails. These tools of themselves are not evil, but the villain lies in the way people employ them to manipulate others, or to hide their identities. The dangers loom largely when digital talk replaces face-to-face communication.

Dating websites are good stages for 'players' to perform their craft; and in order to make profits, the creators of these dating platforms constantly flash their 'success stories' as a means to draw you onto the web; but they never tell you about the mismatches that have disheartened many hopeful women and wreaked innocent lives.

When you negotiate a relationship via the internet, extensive communication and commitment often ensue before the couple meets personally. Naturally, an anxious girl who dates a man on the internet will easily fall for him, inasmuch as she has not met him in person. Moreover, at an arranged get-together, both parties arrive with a predisposition to cement the relationship rather than to assess it; and this sort of negotiation disposes you to danger.

Marriage is the most sacred of human relationships, and therefore its negotiation necessitates extreme vigilance. The observation that the number of seeking women exceeds eligible men gives men the advantage to finding spouses. Why then do men need to employ the internet? Some folk immediately become suspicious that such men are queer, lack chivalry, or are simply playing on women's vulnerabilities.

I believe that when girls advertise via the internet, roles reverse—they become aggressors (to some degree), and sensing their frustration, men take advantage of them. Internet advertisements also have a dehumanizing effect, because they equate women to material merchandize.

True love develops healthier when it ignites from an unpremeditated chemistry between a man and a woman, than through other artificial means that place prerequisites, such as education and occupation, at higher priority than natural appeal. Although the former considerations are critical, they should not supersede the spontaneous attraction that combust when a boy meets a girl in person. Given that you 'shop' online, the very task of scrolling through a stockpile of personal profiles can easily conceal a real 'diamond', but highlight mock samples. However, if you happen to meet someone thereon, try to meet him in person as promptly as possible in order to avoid a fantasy trap. Thus, although digital ads might help you to meet a potential partner, they certainly lack the thrill of a pleasant smile, the warmth of a hug, and the delight of an innocent blush.

"Should I tell my date all about my past?"

4 Questions about Your Past.

Leaving questions about your past life to happenstance is risky; therefore, premeditate beforehand how you will respond. The general approach is to squelch unwarranted details and graphic descriptions of past incidents, because such revelations can incite jealousy. Some men think that it is ok for them to have experience, but experience makes a woman whorish. No woman likes to have her former life screen-played, and therefore, a man should not attempt to squeeze involuntary confessions out of her. On the other hand, if he illustrates episodes with women whom he dated previously, you can underplay their relevance to your acceptance of him, thereby insinuating a similar treatment of your past. Intrusive questions are often pretexts for letting you off, so be careful not to over-commit yourself to a man who concentrates more on the past, than on the present or the future. Moreover, if you keep your date in chase mode, he would scarcely be hypercritical of your history.

Please note that the cautionary advice that I offer repeatedly should not scare you from falling in love, or from trusting others. You must keep a positive opinion of your admirer's intentions--as much as his sincerity motivates, and give him a fair opportunity to serenade you, however, keep a small antenna out to detect possible attempts of unfair play.

Open-ended questions from men can motivate women to over-talk, thereby causing them to reveal unwarranted personal data. It is therefore wise to unfurl yourself gradually--through conduct than through pure rhetoric, least your date become instantaneously knowledgeable of your entire life story, and leaving nothing new to learn about you.

At times, you might even find it shrewd to respond to open-ended questions with correlated subject material. For instance if he questions you regarding your personality, you can roll the dialogue to favorite dishes, or popular vacation venues. This shifts the beam away from your personality onto things that he can readily relate to, and it stirs him to know more about you.

"I'll try that. Now let me ask you another question. Men often like to shower women with compliments—to their advantage—it seems. How should I handle male flattery?"

I believe that every woman finds it thrilling

to hear nice things about her, but she must be wise enough to distinguish genuine compliments from those that are specifically cooked-up to brainwash or entice her.

Men often use flattery to charm women, while they loathe being bantered, therefore, inasmuch as you ought to show appreciation for your date's compliments, you should not let such compliments paralyze you psychologically.

Moreover, your life does not have to be an open book that others can readily read. A sprinkle of mystique sharpens your date's wooing wits and tickles his appetite for more.

One cautionary advice: a girl should never hound a man--only preying animals attack hunters. Remember, you are the game, and he is the huntsman; let him hunt you!

"I find men to be different than women in

many ways, and I also observe that some men are not always willing to accommodate ideas from women. Do you agree?"

5 How Men and Women Differ

There are some differences between each gender—particularly with respect to their approach towards adventure. Men focus chiefly on the prospects of experimentation, whereas women look at the effects that those experiments can yield. Though I agree that some men are downright inflexible when it comes to accepting other people's perspectives, the observation that they show little regard for women's opinions begs the suggestion that friendship should not curb freedom of expression or action. Probably your expectations of cooperation is conflicted with men's ideals of independence, therefore greater tolerance on your part might accommodate for such seeming lack of thoughtfulness. Believing that a couple should always see eye to eye on every subject, or that each party must unquestionably comply with the other person's wishes, is outlandish. No one holds property ownership to another person's life. Thus, relationships thrive best in an atmosphere of freedom and mutual respect.

Men and women differ also when it comes to sexual instinct. A man rouses sexually by physical revelation, and naively, he is like an inquisitive cat whose cravings quench easily once you satisfy them.

A girl, on the other hand, initially attracts to a man mentally, but if she sleeps with him, a physical attachment forms easily, due to the release of ecstasy hormones. This explains why men—unlike women--can walk away from relationships without experiencing emotional hang-ups. Worse yet, a girl can even become addicted to an abusive man, whose sexual thrill and companionship she fears loosing. Under such circumstance, although she knows that the relationship is toxic, she lacks the energy to extricate herself. Let me take you on an imaginary trip to the zoo. Imagine two chipmunks perching on the branch of a barren tree that stands close to a fruit laden one. Both chipmunks gaze across and behold the luscious fruits, but the rodents can only get to them by letting go of the barren branch and leaping onto to the fruit laden ones. One brave chipmunk unfurls his grasp from the barren branch and leaps onto the fruit laden tree where he partakes of the luscious fruits. However, the uncourageous chipmunk dare not let go of the branch that supports him, but tries reaching across with one hand whilst still grasping the barren branch with the other. However, the fruit laden tree is beyond his clutch. "Let go and jump", yells the courageous chipmunk, but the cowardly chipmunk never musters the nerve to leap, so he remains on the barren tree and starves to death, while the brave chipmunk feasts sumptuously on the delicious fruits.

"Interesting chipmunk story! So, some women keep holding on to toxic relationship for fear of not securing another?

Yep! Sometimes you have to let go and leap away from a bad relationship in order to catch a good one. People in general—men and women—prefer to secure a new friendship before they let go of a noxious one, simply because they fear aloneness. However, some risks are worth taking.

Contrary to being a curiosity creature, a girl's personality is drizzled with sentimentalism. She tends often to dream of a glamorous wedding; she can become enraptured with its trappings and put her man backstage, until when she wakes up from her dream one day, she finds herself lying beside a stranger for failure to know the man who knelt before her and slid a diamond on her finger.

Men and women fall in love differently also, and they mature at different ages and stages in their lives. Women reach maturity earlier than men do, and they are generally more disposed to hitch at younger ages. Therefore, another critical element to consider when seeking for a soul mate is the person's state of readiness. Good provider and nurturer type men usually reach marriageable readiness after completing their education and securing a decent job, but evasive men are unpredictable and might never commit— regardless of your waiting tolerance.

Men differ from women emotionally as well. "Big boys don't cry," thumped their eardrums over the years, so men got conditioning to repress their feelings and emotions; and these suppressions made them less capable to feel empathy, articulate their feelings, and experience guilt—all handicaps to forming and maintaining love relationships. If men could learn to express their true feelings, and be willing to accept and process women's, they would be better partners.

"I agree!"

Emotional intimacy breeds trust, and trust begets love—a kind of domino effect. This is risky—I admit, but it yields good fruit in the long term.

Another good relationship strategy is to readily acknowledge your mistakes and apologize to your partner before such disagreements escalate into bush fires. Frankness to accept others for who they are--and not who you wish them to be, is important. Do not forget that the faults we find in others are often projections of ours.

"Let me ask another question: Should I be

worried if my date is seeing someone else?"

Worrying unduly over your date's social life, or nagging him if you have a slight suspicion that he's cheating on you lowers your self-assurance and pushes him closer to your competitor; but calmness communicates a trust that can cause him to retract. However, if he leaves you for her, then you were not right for each other in the first instance. Putting it in jingle: it is better to remain single than to marry the devil.

"Ok, if I happen to meet a great guy, and I'm reasonably sure that he will marry me, is it ok to sleep with him in the meantime?"

Let's talk about that.

6 How Soon to Sleep Together?

Surrendering yourself prematurely to a man's romantic solicitations has two spokes: first, it means to communicate the emotion that you adore him, and second, that you have no specific boundaries of intimacy. However, there is an alternative. You can deter his moves artistically without wounding his enthusiasm. Responding to his moves with remarks such as, "I am not ready for this yet", "this is not the right time", "we barely know each other", "you are moving much too fast for me" can help to keep him in check. These answers differ from a cold NO, because they infer the possibility of sexual familiarity sometime in the future—ideally after marriage. You might be tempted to believe that he would regard you as weird for putting him off; but in fact, you are the pedigree of woman that good men are looking for, because you are different from average ones. The girl who knows herself, what she is looking for in a relationship, what she permits, and the type of man she is looking for, is also the kind of girl who makes a good wife, and men are aware of these things.

"Continue"

It is illusive to think that you can test-drive as many men as possible, then park (settle down) whenever you meet the right model. By then, you may become addicted to a multi-sexual lifestyle, and might find it difficult (or impossible) to direct your affections exclusively on Mr. Right even after you are married, let alone the embarrassment of encountering former bed partners.

Auditioning does greater harm to girls than it does to men, because male and female sexuality differ technically. A man's initial urge is instinctively biological—much like an animal's, whereas a woman's is emotional. Her desires originate from an innate yearning to receive love and affection, though at times she substitutes the sexual act for the love she hungers for, thereby plunging herself deeper into emotional insecurity. Rather than enabling you to make good choices, or what constitutes a good character, auditioning confuses you to the point of questioning your personal identity. Advanced auditioning (co-habiting) is even riskier. Co-habiting girls are mostly the evasive types who fear emotional exposure, and/or divorce; but observations attest that co-habiting couples usually do not remain married long after they have tied the knot. Why? Having tried every 'trick in the hat' prior to the wedding leaves nothing new to explore. Thence, for many couples who engaged sexually during courtship, marriage often degenerates into a drudge.

Girls opt to become sexually active for several reasons: to validate their sexuality, as a stunt to outwit their female competitors, as an anesthesia for emotional injury, as a means to inflict revenge on a cheating boyfriend, as a hypnotic potion to entice men, or simply as conformity to modern sexology myth. In all such instances, the price is irremediable, and the consequences generally counter-productive to a healthy marriage.

Sexual bribery yields unanticipated results. The man, whom a seductive girl attempts to entice, loses interest in her, and may dismiss her in preference for another one who clearly defines her boundaries. Moreover, men naturally tend to be disdainful towards women whom they have slept with, but with whom they lack emotional connectivity. If good looks and sex were capable of binding people, then men would not leave their beautiful wives for less gorgeous women, nor would women for less handsome men.

Sex is high-risk business for women. Pregnancy, death during childbirth, sexually transmitted infections, and single parenthood, are some of the 'demons' that women dare by consenting to premarital sex, but these threats reduce significantly whenever copulation occurs within the harbor of a trustful monogamous relationship—marriage ideally.

Additionally, premarital sex puts your relationship on steroids and accelerates it to uncontrollable velocities, thereby escalating the odds of a wreck. Moreover, it is a huge non-refundable price to pay for a bouquet of sugarcoated promises.

Evidences attest that sex does not manufacture love—it merely celebrates the love that already exists. If it were a relationship booster, there would be many less lonely women looking to find true love. In fact, couples who celebrate sex after marriage, and are exclusively faithful to each other, live longer and happier lives than sexually indiscriminate ones.

"Carlisle, the majority of people do not wait! Abstinence requires enormous self-control. How can I restrain myself if I feel strongly in love with the man I'm dating?"

There is a difference between *feeling* that you are in love, and *being* in love. Facts and feelings do not always harmonize. Love should be validated through demonstrations of trust and commitment— not by a bunch of flapping butterflies in the stomach, or an ecstasy hormone rush. Love is patient, but infatuation (love's counterfeit) hastens to raid private property; therefore be on guard for 'hunters' who aim to take down prey at close range.

Denying intercourse prior to marriage is not an easy victory to win, I admit, but it is achievable. The discipline of waiting is the same as what is required to sustain the relationship after the wedding. Failure to control sexual urges inevitably weakens the ability to maintain loyalty during wedlock, but self-control facilitates fidelity and permanence. Sex is similar to a Christmas gift, which, if opened prematurely, ruins the excitement that Christmas morning unwrapping emotes. Worse yet, guilt and regret most often mock self-worth, particularly if the relationship dissolves unexpectedly.

A well-intentioned man wants to know that his mate is not a softie who surrenders easily to men's charms. A man may flirt with a thousand women, but when ready to nest, he chooses the most resistant one. In fact, I believe that a man thinks twice before marrying a sexually experienced woman, because such realization wounds his pride of not being 'Mister Only'. However, if he marries her eventually, the quality of respect, which he construes that her qualifications merit, can possibly hamper his commitment to her.

"How can I put off a man whom I have feelings for, and who believes that sex is a normal act of courtship?"

One secret of preventing premarital sex is to avoid environments and circumstances that lower your guard, or that gives your date an advantage to fondle. Public places such as shopping malls, libraries, busy parks, and museums are good dating venues, because they provide a measure of safety against premature moves on you. Going to his home to view the oil paintings on his wall is not an intelligent choice.

Boarding a flight will only take you flying, and warming-up on the tracks prepares you for running. Just so, permitting a little play might take you to the finish line.

Realizing how difficult it is to think rationally when your romantic energy surges into high tide, you need to arm yourself with some lust-busters for disabling romantic dizziness. Marriages cast on sexual stimuli stand the risk of crumbling as swiftly as the frisky thrills evaporate, because sex of itself lacks the spine to support the weights that will bear upon your marriage afterwards.

The intrusion of sex during the delicate bonding phase chokes communication, and strands of love that might have glowed, singe easily by fiery lusts that swiftly blaze, dwindle, then stifle altogether, almost as hastily as they sparkled.

Keeping silent when your partner makes a move on you will only invite further exploration, but a sobering conversation can quickly subdue lust. This is what you can try. Take a deep breath, relax, smile, disengage yourself from any uncomfortable state, and then throw one of your preplanned questions to steer him back onto a sober track.

"Carlisle, what happens to people when they begin to fall in love?"

Love evolves through a series of stages before blooming into the elegant flower of lasting commitment. Initially, it constitutes an excitement at the sight and sound of the other person. We can call this the 'butterfly-in-the-stomach' stage, which thrills register emotionally in the girl's mind—a process which active communication further fuels. For such reason, several marriage counselors advocate a slow approach to falling in love.

Thence onwards, the relationship can take

two different directions—either the circuitous verbal communication route, which gives you time to think, assess, and change your mind; or a physical fantasy cruise that quickly merges onto a romantic frenzied lane, whereupon the couple never seems to have enough of each other. We might name this the 'infatuation-detour' stage.

However, soon thereafter, sobering concerns--like money, education, future goals, and family life parade the thoughts, and the gleeful butterflies disappear. This is the wake-up stage where each one begins to see the other person's faults; and the direction veered at this crossroad can etch a girl's fortune.

The physical infatuation grasp has the muscle to cripple your mind into making subjective choices, such as marrying a man whom you latch onto physically, but lack spiritual and emotional bond with.

Therefore, if in the first instance you resisted the drag of lust, you might walk away a free woman, but not easily so if you are sexually involved with that man, because sex is addictive, and it can bind you involuntarily to one whom commonsense screams to wave goodbye to.

In a similar manner that hunters relish game that they have vigilantly pursued, men, who are love hunters, are more passionate for women whom they chase after. Therefore, the longer you can keep a man passionately suspended, with his heart turned-on and his hands off, the more thrilling the courtship experience can be.

On the contrary, a man interprets easy surrender as a symptom of desperation, and so he takes advantage of your charity then goes elsewhere to conquer new landscape. Setting boundaries of physical intimacy will not cause a man to leave you if he is genuinely attracted to your inner beauty; it merely intensifies his passion to draw closer.

Moreover, during the initial stages of a relationship, if a man remains partly uncertain of your feelings for him, he will try more convincingly to persuade you that he truly cares. This feels good—I imagine. Remember, Mister Right's wooing efforts match your merit, so keep him chasing all the way to the chapel.

To tell what often happens when physical attraction is the premier ingredient of a relationship, or when a friendship accelerates too fast, I will give personalities to some of the players in the love game.

If, on a love boat cruise, lust and sex come aboard whilst commitment and marriage are yet to arrive, the aggressive couple (lust and sex) dominates relationship to the point that it first becomes intoxicated, stuns sometime later, and then pines. Without marriage and love onboard to maintain relationship's balance, sex's wooziness causes it to pass out completely, leaving broken heart to clean up the muddle, mend the fragments, learn, and then seek to find true love again.

"It's not so easy to love again if I were hurt like that?"

I agree; but an awful experience should never make you callous. You must continue to live and love—no matter what. According to the Bible (Genesis Chapter 29), after craftily handed the wrong bride—Leah, Jacob waited and worked another seven years for Rachel—the one he truly loved. Though deceived at first, he finally found his love.

"Question! According to popular stats, about fifty percent of all marriages end in divorce. If I manage to meet and marry a terrific guy, what can I do to make sure that we remain happily married?

The mere fact that divorce is so rampant suggests that keeping relationships intact presents greater challenges than forming them. Though incompatibility and impetuous decisions account for a significant percentage of divorces, the rest are direct consequences of the parties' inability to sustain healthy relationships. People simply do not put enough work into keeping love alive; they presume marriage to be a magic potion for curing the 'sickness' of singleness. However, marriage is only the beginning of a journey fraught with bumps, and twist and turns. Soon after the wedding, you will find your husband to be naively different from the character you shortly fell in love with. Yep! Women change as well. Nevertheless, compliment him on those rare occasions that he does something right. Men have a basic need to get respect, whereas women need love and affection.

Cynicism has a creepy way of rebounding

on its donor; what hurts your partner will inevitably hurt your marriage. There are a few things that you must be particularly careful about, which are also equally relevant to men.

First, do not nag your spouse. Disagreements are inevitable, but deal with the problem and avoid making generalized derogatory statements regarding his person. Do not adduce past records to prove your correctness on a current subject; attend to matters as they arise, and when settled, discard them permanently.

Secondly, be a good listener. I have seldom witnessed a good dialogue between two persons with a disagreement. What I have seen instead is both parties taking turns at monologues; no one listens to the other, but only interrupts to say one's piece. Sadly, many of these discrepancies escalate to the point of separation. If people listened more and talked less, the world's quarrels and divorces can probably shrink by more than half.

Thirdly, communicate on a deep level with your husband. Women commonly hold the notion that most men leave for other women's bodies; but this does not hold true in the majority of cases—even though voluptuousness can initially enamor them. Mental connectivity bonds stronger than warm bodies; the thrills of physical ecstasy quickly evaporate as bodies cool off.

Fourthly, although you must set up family rituals, and spend quality time together, keep some girly things going for you, that is, some of the things that you enjoyed while growing up—wholesome pleasures of course, which are mutually agreed upon. Similarly, allow him to have fun doing things he enjoys, like sports, or fixing cars, etcetera. A little 'breathing-space' can prevent relationship fermentation.

Fifthly, keep up that attractive look that

caught his attention in the first instance. Numerous women merely slump into a housekeeper's posture once they are married, only to have their husbands' attention diverted elsewhere. I am not giving licenses to men to look outside of marriage when their wives' luster mask by the grind of home chores, but most men like to see their wives looking pretty as ever they met them. Therefore, if you have to get dirty during the day, beauty-up when he is about to arrive.

"Let's not get carried away here. I have not even found a guy yet, but we are discussing how to keep a good relationship with one."

Don't worry; you'd be just fine.

"Ok, so I'm ready to go hunting.

Hunting! Remember you are the game and he is the huntsman; let him find you. All you need to do is work on improving your self-esteem, present yourself elegantly, dress conservatively, control your passions, be a lady, and participate in exciting social and educational activities, and then you would be able to wow a terrific guy who will love and marry you, and then bring you roses forever. Best wishes!

Conclusion

About two months later when I met her, she was radiating a new excitement. Apparently, the suggestions had helped her in a practical way, and I believe that she is now on the right path to attract an adorable man who will love her for the rest of her life.

ABOUT THE AUTHOR

Carlisle has been married since nineteen hundred and eighty, and as a father, husband, and youth leader, he has often counseled young people in the area of relationships. Having three daughters, he hates to see young women exploited by men, and therefore he delights to offer encouragement and advice to those who are seeking meaningful relationships. The practical suggestions that he offers stem specifically from observations and personal experiences over the past.

Carlisle hopes that the contents of this book will give young women some handles on managing relationships and making correct assessments of men, and that by so doing, women will experience the joys in life that God intended them to enjoy.